S

N

G

Y

BRENT LIBRARIES

Please return/renew this item
by the last date shown.
Books may also be renewed by
phone or online.
Tel: 0115 929 3388
On-line www.brent.gov.uk/libraryservice

First published in paperback in 2014 by Wayland

Text copyright © Claire Llewellyn 2014
Illustrations copyright © Mike Gordon 2014

Wayland
338 Euston Road
London NW1 3BH

Wayland Australia
Level 17/207 Kent Street
Sydney, NSW 2000

Senior editor: Camilla Lloyd
Designer: Paul Cherrill
Digital Colour: Carl Gordon

British Library Cataloguing in Publication Data:
Llewellyn, Claire.
Spending my money. -- (Your money!)
1. Money--Juvenile literature. 2. Finance, Personal--Juvenile literature.
I. Title II. Series III. Gordon, Mike, 1948 Mar. 16-
332'.024-dc22

ISBN: 978 0 7502 8871 2

Printed in China

First published in 2010 by Wayland

Wayland is a division of Hachette Children's Books, an Hachette UK company.

www.hachette.co.uk

SPENDING MY MONEY

Written by
Claire Llewellyn

Illustrated by
Mike Gordon

WAYLAND

We all go shopping now and again – for food, clothes, or something for the home.

5

First, we have to find what we want.

Then we have to pay
for it. We have to give
the shop some money.

We pay for things in different ways. We can use real money – in other words, notes and coins.

But money is
bulky and easy
to lose.

So most grown-ups keep their
money in the bank and pay
with a bank card instead.

A what card?

A bank card is a special plastic card.
It lets grown-ups pay for things without
using notes and coins.

And they can use it to get real money
out of cash machines, too.

Spending money can make you feel good if you're happy with the things you buy.

But sometimes you can feel let down.

You wish you hadn't spent your money after all.

But remember, shopping isn't the only way you can spend money.

You can also give it to charity.

You can do a lot with money.

20

So try not to waste it on the wrong thing, and always spend your money WELL.

Notes For Parents and Teachers

We all need to be able to manage our money and make financial decisions. The four books in the 'Your Money' series are intended as a first step along this path. Based on children's everyday lives, the series is a light-hearted introduction to money, everyday financial transactions, planning and saving and financial choices.

'Spending my Money' discusses our day-to-day handling of money in paying for goods and services. It compares paying in cash with using a bank card. It explores the positive or negative reactions we sometimes have to our purchases, and discusses giving money to charity as another form of 'spending'.

Suggested follow-up activities

• When you go shopping, talk to your child about how you are paying. Are you paying in cash or with plastic? If you are paying with a card, explain you are using money that you have earned and stored in the bank. If you are getting 'cash-back', explain how this works.

• Next time you are in a supermarket, ask your child to find out the cost of three of their favourite foods.

• Play a game of money bingo. First make a template card with six blank squares, and photocopy them. Now fill in the blank squares with different numbers below 100 that are from the ten times table.

Give each player a bingo card and six counters. The bingo caller calls out an amount from the ten times table (e.g. £30). Players must use a counter to cover the number that would add up to £100 with the amount called. In the above example, this would be £70.

• Give children a bank card to examine. Show them that it has a name on it and a lot of numbers that belong to a bank account — a kind of moneybox where people store their money. Look at other features on the card, including the signature and the computer chip and explain what these are for.

• Talk to your child about how you use a bank card to get money out of a cash machine. Tell them there is a code to stop other people using the card. The code is a secret four-digit number. If the child had a card, which code would they choose and why?

• Talk with the children about the best and worst purchases they have ever made (or had made for them). For example, was it something they asked for for their birthday that they were disappointed with? Or something unexpected that they really love? Tell them about some of the good and bad purchases you have made yourself.

• Next time you are out with your child and give to a charity collection, ask the collector what the money will be used for and how it helps the cause.

BOOKS TO READ

'Money Doesn't Grow on Trees' by Paul Mason (Wayland, 2014)
'Lots and Lots of Coins' by Margarette S Reid (Puffin Books, 2014)
'Using Money' by Rebecca Rissman (Heinemann Library, 2010)

USEFUL WEBSITES

www.pfeg.org

INDEX